This book belongs to:

____

Made in the USA
Middletown, DE
30 November 2019

79570785R00066